Al

KITTEN AND CAT CARE

Patricia Paula

Photography: Glen Axelrod, Isabelle Francais, and Robert [...]

© T.F.H. Publications, Inc.

[dis]tributed in the UNITED STATES to the Pet Trade by T.F.H. Publications, Inc., 1 TFH Plaza, Neptune City, NJ 07753; [on] the Internet at www.tfh.com; in CANADA by Rolf C. Hagen Inc., 3225 Sartelon St., Montreal, Quebec H4R 1E8; [Pe]t Trade by H & L Pet Supplies Inc., 27 Kingston Crescent, Kitchener, Ontario N2B 2T6; in ENGLAND by T.F.H. [Pu]blications, PO Box 74, Havant PO9 5TT; in AUSTRALIA AND THE SOUTH PACIFIC by T.F.H. (Australia), Pty. Ltd., [Bo]x 149, Brookvale 2100 N.S.W., Australia; in NEW ZEALAND by Brooklands Aquarium Ltd., 5 McGiven Drive, New [Ply]mouth, RD1 New Zealand; in SOUTH AFRICA by Rolf C. Hagen S.A. (PTY.) LTD., P.O. Box 201199, Durban North [40]16, South Africa; in JAPAN by T.F.H. Publications. Published by T.F.H. Publications, Inc.
MANUFACTURED IN THE
UNITED STATES OF AMERICA
BY T.F.H. PUBLICATIONS, INC.

USA 22

Siamese Cat, Exotic Shorthair Cat

USA 22

Abyssinian Cat, Himalayan Cat

USA 22

Maine Coon Cat, Burmese Cat

USA 22

American Shorthair Cat, Persian Cat

USA 22

Siamese Cat, Exotic Shorthair Cat

USA 22

Abyssinian Cat, Himalayan Cat

USA 22

Maine Coon Cat, Burmese Cat

USA 22

American Shorthair Cat, Persian Cat

Commemorative cat stamps issued in the 1980s.

CONTENTS

This Siamese-like mixed breed is enjoying the attention of its young owner. Cats can make great pets for people of all ages.

THE CAT AS A PET

The fact that you have ked up this book on do-stic cats and kittens would dicate that you are inter-ed in finding out a little re about these elegant mbers of the family Fel-e. You are not alone. At s time, cats and kittens ve become one of the most sirable of all pets. Everyone familiar with the cat; it is, er all, a very common pet d can be seen roaming the eys and streets of most ge cities. Why then has it ddenly become so desir-le? In a nutshell, the an-er to this question is the t that it is the most conve-nt of all the pets from ich you can choose. This is the starting point; t, once acquired, people on begin to appreciate the merous virtues of these lividualistic predators. They e sensitive creatures born of ew hundred generations of imals that have had a very xed relationship with us mans. Totally different m the dog in their attitude life, they pay homage to no e, including their owner. ey are essentially loners at will happily share your me with you on a mutually rkable basis. For your part, u will provide their food, see at they are nicely groomed, d provide a warm, comfy ace for them to sleep. If they come ill, you will see that ey receive the correct terinary treatment, and of urse you will allow them the al freedom of your house. r their part, they will favor

you by staying to enjoy these benefits! This is the cat.

Now you may think that this seems a pretty one-sided arrangement, but this is why the cat is such a sophisticated pet. If you do not live up to your part, then do not expect your cat to be around too long: it will sooner or later

terrorizing the neighborhood as might a large dog left to its own devices, nor will it howl and bark when left at home. Cats like being indoors, and there's far fewer dangers in your home than there are outdoors.

You will not need an array of expensive equipment to

Some cats are more responsive to people than are others; some will have a favorite person among the members of their human family.

find someone else more appreciative of its presence. If not, it will return to the wild side and look after its own welfare, something cats have been doing very well through-out their evolution.

The very independent nature of the cat is the basis of its sheer convenience. You will not need to take it for a walk, for roaming around the house is more than enough exercise. It will not go out

own a cat as you would if you decided to keep tropical fish, nor will you need to reduce the pet to a virtual prisoner by caging it as you would with rabbits, guinea pigs, ham-sters, or birds. In the cat, you have a pet that can be given total freedom, yet will happily stay with you, and at the same time not be regarded as a nuisance or a threat to other people in your neighbor-hood.

Your kitten, and the cat it grows up to become, will not cost you a fortune to feed, its housing needs are simplicity itself. Even the cost of the kitten need not be more than a modest sum if you decide to own a non-purebred. If you give your kitten a great deal of affection, this will be returned in kind. It will happily curl up on your lap and purr contentedly. It will amuse you with its antics and its superb jumping and acrobatic abilities. A kitten really is the most comical of pets and it finds pleasure in the simplest of articles to play with.

own thing. It is impossible to say which sort of cat you will acquire because they are not as predictable as dogs. They are harder to fathom at times, yet this is part of their appeal. Some are very lazy, others very active. For these reasons, once hooked on them, most owners will end up with two or more felines.

With a cat and a kitten, what you see is what you get. While a little puppy may grow up to be a veritable giant, this will never happen with your kitten. All cats stay within very tolerable size limits, so, from a management viewpoint, you

you will have more than enough to choose from. You can also have a kitten in one of a number of fur types: lon medium, short, curly, or, if the unusual appeals to you even one with virtually no hair. Most cats have a long tail, but there are breeds with short tails, and one that may have no tail at all There two breeds with unusual ears, one having the folded and the other with curled ears. However, it is best to select from cats tha are essentially as nature intended them to be; this, after all, ensures that they

You will find that when a cat moves in, most sensible mice move out, so there is a practical benefit in owning a cat. Some cats will follow you around your home, constantly seeking your attention and always wanting to be with you. Some will enjoy walking with you around your garden; others will prefer to do their

A scratching post and toys are a must for every cat-owning household.

are assured that your kitten will not grow to a size that you did not anticipate.

The potential range of color and coat pattern combinations in cats is enormous, so

will be less prone to health problems.

If the idea of breeding and exhibiting cats appeals to yo then you will find there is a large and well-established hobby based upon just this aspect. Indeed, the hobby ha grown to such an extent tha there are a few people who make a full-time living from

American Shorthair kittens. The distinctive markings above the eyes are characteristic of the breed.

Youngsters should be taught early on about how to properly handle the family cat. Caring for a pet can help to teach a child a sense of responsibility.

the cat as a pet

eeding and showing their
ock. However, working up to
ch a level is a costly and
me-consuming business.
ost breeders and exhibitors
volve themselves purely as a
stime.

Although cats are essen-
ally loners when out and
out, they are nonetheless
r more social than was
ought for many years. This
, they will certainly enjoy

apartment and house renters,
forbid the owning of dogs,
they will accept cats. This
reflects the unobtrusive and
quiet nature of these stealthy
animals. Given all the virtues
of cats and kittens, you may
be wondering if they have any
faults. It would be misleading
to say they are all angels.
Many will catch and kill most
rodents from mice to squir-
rels, and they will not shy

life. You cannot train them as
you can a dog, so don't expect
them to come to your bid and
call like some benign servant.
They will come if they feel so
disposed, and generally they
will if they are in a loving
home, and especially at meal
times! Kittens are easy to
litter train, and providing they
have access to a scratching
post they will not damage
your furniture. They certainly

e company of their own kind
your home. I would say
thout hesitation that if you
e thinking of having a
ten, you cannot go wrong
having two. They are little
ore trouble to look after and
ll provide you with a con-
ant source of companionship
d amusement.

You will find that while
any government housing
ojects, as well as many

**Lilac Siamese and blue cream
Balinese. In essence, the
Balinese is a Siamese in a
longhaired coat.**

away from bringing these
home to you, along with any
birds that they can pounce
on. This predatory aspect of
their nature may not appeal
to every person, but with such
a born hunter it is a fact of

will not bite pieces out of it as
dogs may sometimes do if not
trained.

With a cat, you have the
rare opportunity of having in
your home a lion or leopard in
miniature. This is an animal
that is only partially domesti-
cated in many instances. It
can as easily return to the
wild and survive as it can
settle for a more comfortable
existence in your company.

the cat as a pet

There are not many pets that this can be said of. Whether f the young, or the more elderl; kittens and cats are truly adorable pets that will fit in with your daily routine with r problem at all. They make few demands on you and actually offer a great deal in return.

If you already own a dog, a rabbit, or other pets larger, o almost as large as a cat, ther you will find that a feline will quickly become a friend to them, the more so if you obta a kitten. Throughout this introduction to the cat, you will note that I have stressed that it is a more convenient p than any other popular animal. This does not suggest it is a better pet than a dog or parrot, because such judgments, of necessity, can only be determined on a personal basis. If you are looking for a pet that can live in your home that will be an affectionate companion, yet will not be intrusive by its presence, ther a cat a is very good choice.

Top: The Siamese is one of the most popular breeds in the cat fancy. The points—face mask, ears, paws, and tail—come in four different colors: chocolate, blue, lilac, and seal, which is shown here. Bottom: American Bobtail. This cat is a relative newcomer among the bobtailed breeds. It is known for its lively, intelligent personality.

WHAT WILL THE CAT NEED?

One of the considerable advantages in owning a cat is the fact that there are actually very few items that are needed in order to care for it in a home environment. A number of them could be supplied from items you probably have in the house already. This said, most owners will prefer to purchase at least some basic articles specifically for their new companion. The range of equipment made for cats is extensive. Here we can review some of those that will be needed in one form or another.

CAT CARRIER

This is an item that often proves extremely handy over the years. It is needed when taking the cat to the vet, or when there is a need to confine it, or when a home move is in the cards. It is essential if you like to take the kitten or cat on vacation with you. If you decide to exhibit your cats, then of course it is mandatory that one or more cat carriers are owned. Be sure that the one chosen will be large enough for the adult cat; otherwise, you will have to purchase another one at a later date. It should be strong, well supplied with ventilation holes, and have a secure means of fastening it. If you are likely to travel a lot, then invest in the biggest and best one that you can find.

SCRATCHING POST

In order to remove the possibility of the cat scratching your furniture, it is best

A cat travel bag will enable you to transport your cat safely and comfortably. Photo courtesy of Sherpa's Pet Trading Company.

to obtain a good scratching post. This may be a freestanding unit, or one which is screwed to the wall. Pet shops stock a variety of scratching posts. A lightweight ball attached to a piece of string can be suspended from the top of the post. This will encourage the kitten to play, and thus use the post.

LITTER TRAY

Cats are extremely clean pets and will foul your home only if they have no means of doing otherwise. A litter tray is essential for a kitten, which cannot control its bowel movements for more than a few seconds. Plastic trays are available from your pet shop. Purchase the larger ones, ideally those with raised removable sides that will prevent the litter from being

scattered over the floor. Initially, this add-on piece may not be needed because the kitten will be small. It is useful as kitty becomes a cat—especially with those who take the job of covering fecal matter extremely seriously and spend ages attending to this. You can purchase igloo types, which have a covered top which reduces, or restricts, the odors created. However, most of the better brands of cat litter are impregnated with an odor absorber. You will need a plastic scoop to remove litter and fecal matter, because cats do not like to use an already fouled tray. If it is not kept clean, this will merely discourage the cat from using it; thus it may be forced to attend to its toiletry needs elsewhere in the house.

what will the cat need?

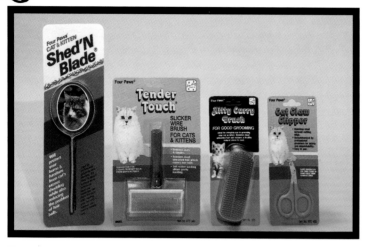

Your cat should be groomed on a regular basis. From brushes to nail clippers, your pet shop will meet your pet's every grooming need. Photo courtesy of Four Paws.

FOOD AND WATER DISHES

There is a wide selection of dishes, mostly in plastic, that can be obtained for cats. Earthenware (crock) and aluminum are more costly but longer lasting. You could use saucers for the food, and these are actually as good as any special dishes because you are not likely to be tempted to pile too much food onto them. This is better because cats are ideally fed little and often, rather than having a dish full which they will not always eat, and which will thus attract flies and start to go dry.

CAT COLLAR AND ID TAG

Collars for cats must be elasticized to reduce the risk of the kitten or cat becoming caught up on a branch when it is out and about. The ID tag, which should bear your name, address, and phone number, is an obvious need in case the cat gets lost. Some collars have bells fitted to them so it is not as easy for the cat to catch mice, birds and the like. However, these

Right: Lilac point Birman. Regular grooming is especially important with the longhaired breeds. In addition to keeping your cat looking its best, it can help to prevent skin and coat problems. Below: This stylish scratching post features several perches, as well as an enclosure at the bottom.

are not successful if the cat a skilled hunter.

If you plan to take your kitten with you on vacation, or short trips, you might consider the purchase of a c harness, additional to its collar. It must be made for cats and not small dogs. Mo are of a nylon material so th are very light. The harness gives you a little more contro over the cat in the event tha it is startled and attempts to back out of its collar. Cats d not like walking on a collar/ harness and lead but some, especially those of foreign type, take to it more readily, particularly if they are traine to this from kittenhood.

GROOMING AIDS

The grooming tools that y will need for your kitten will be determined by its coat length. Shorthaired cats require only a brush and a medium/fine toothed comb. For longhaired breeds, you may find the double-sided brush with pins on one side and bristles on the other a useful addition. You can also purchase rubber curry-type combs that are not as severe on the coat as those with win pins. Bristle brushes and steel combs are preferred to plastic, as the latter creates lot of static electricity in longhaired coats. A pair of curved and blunt-ended scissors may also be useful

tidying up the long hairs the feet of longhaired eeds.

T BEDS

There is a good choice of beds available for cats. ey are made of wicker, astic, canvas, wood, or erglass. The chosen bed ould be easy to clean, ich makes fiberglass an cellent choice. Although me cats will use a bed, most ose not to. They would ch rather curl up on the fa, a nice chair, or your bed. ey prefer to be off of the or most of the time when ey go to sleep, so if you do rchase a bed, try to put it an elevated area.

YS AND OTHER ITEMS

Your local pet store will ve a wide range of cat toys m which you can choose. e more sophisticated and pensive playthings, such as

climbing frames covered in carpeting, will provide a lot of enjoyment for kittens and cats—the more so if they have things dangling from them. Cats like to paw at these kinds of toys.

You can purchase such things as playpens, or heating pads for the kitty's bed, but these items are not at all necessary. A much better investment would be to purchase a few specialty

books on cats and subjects related to them—maybe one devoted to the particular breed you decide to own. It is always wise to obtain as many of the desired accessories as you can in advance of the arrival day of the kitten or cat. This way, you have more chance to shop around and to be sure everything is on hand when the kitten is eventually introduced to the household.

This youngster keeps careful supervision over his cat when they are outdoors.

Cats aren't choosy about their toys. For this cat, a piece of yarn is as good a toy as any.

CHOOSING A KITTEN OR CAT

Having decided that you are definitely going to obtain a kitten or a cat, there are a number of considerations that a genuine cat lover will need to carefully ponder so that the right choice is made.

KITTEN OR CAT?

For most, but not all, potential owners, a kitten will be the preferred choice. They are really amusing—the more so if you obtain two at the same time. They will provide company for each other while you are out at work. The drawback is that kittens will require a lot more attention than will an adult, and they are more mischievous as well. The adult cat will already be more set in its ways and may be the sort that will wander

It will be much harder to introduce an adult cat into a household that has a dog, but is possible, depending on the nature of the dog more than the cat. Even so, many people, this author's family included, have taken in adults as well as kittens and been very pleased with them. More elderly people may find the adult a better choice. If you are interested in exhibiting or breeding cats, these aspects would influence your choice. In either case, I would suggest the young adult might be the best option. This is because the older kitten/young adult will be more mature, thus its quality will be more readily ascertained. However, such a pet will be rather more expensive. This fact might mean

that you have to take a little more risk and go for a younger animal.

AGE TO PURCHASE

If you have never owned a cat before, then it would be wise to obtain a kitten that is about 10-16 weeks of age. Such a kitten will be more established. In all probability, it will have been vaccinated against the major feline diseases. It is quite possible to rear a kitten from six weeks of age, but this will require your

Nine-week-old chocolate point Siamese kitten.

devoting much more time to it. Generally, such a path is not recommended for the first-time cat owner. With a young adult required for exhibition or breeding, a sound age would be when it is about nine or more months of age.

PUREBRED OR MOGGIE?

Unlike dogs, in which mongrels can grow to be any

size and may look like a really mixed bag, the moggie (mixed breed) cat often looks more beautiful than many purebreds. Their size will not be a factor that you need to ponder because all cats are within a tolerable range. If you plan to breed cats, or to seriously exhibit, a purebred has to be the only choice. Even if you want a cat only as a companion, you may have a particular liking for one of the purebred varieties, and in a particular color.

Bear in mind that cats are currently extremely popular pets and a thriving market has developed for stolen purebred cats, especially kittens. If you are not concerned about the ancestry of your pet, the moggie is possibly the best choice. Or, perhaps you could have one of each type?

COAT TYPE

I would say without hesitation that for the first-time owner, a short- or medium-haired kitten or cat would be the best choice.

Only if you know that you have the time and inclination to devote fifteen or so minutes each day to grooming should you consider the longhaired breeds, such as Persians. Shorthaired breeds need only infrequent brushing because they keep their coats looking immaculate. Persian types will quickly become a mass of tangles if they are not groomed daily. You can always obtain a longhaired breed once you are sure that you are a really dedicated cat lover.

I would also add that for the novice owner, he should restrict his choice to breeds that show no alteration to the basic anatomy of the cat. On this account, breeds with no tail, no hair, or any other genetic alteration to their structure, are best left until experience has been gained with cats. This still leaves you with a considerable range of cats from which to choose— and in all of the colors and patterns known to exist in cats.

MALE OR FEMALE?

If you are having the kitten or cat as a companion only, then it does not matter which sex it is: both sexes are loving and affectionate. If you plan to breed, the queen should be your first choice. Owning a whole (unneutered) tom cat presents many problems. He will be marking his territory

(your home) with his scent– rather unpleasant pungent sort of aroma that I would rank only just a little better than that of a skunk! The latter at least disappears qu quickly, whereas that of the tom is being constantly add to.

The whole tom will be ou and about maintaining his outdoor territory and will be fighting any would-be in- truder more willingly than v the neutered tom. Further, you are to become a breede you will ideally use the ser- vices of a leading stud of proven ability at siring litter and stamping his type on them.

If the kitten or cat is to be solely a pet, then please see that it is neutered. The sma cost involved is worth every penny paid. You will not be hit with a succession of litters.

> A longhaired Scottish Fold sporting beautiful pelage. This breed, which also comes in a shorthaired version, is characterized by its folded ears, which are the result of a mutation.

In the case of the tom, it
[wi]ll not be marking its terri-
[tor]y all of the time, nor land-
[ing] someone else with un-
[wa]nted kittens that end up in
[th]e local animal shelter, or
[wo]rse, being abandoned. It
[ma]kes you wonder about
[pe]ople when cats are disposed
[of] in these ways. You can
[re]duce the incidence of this
[ha]ppening by neutering or
[sp]aying your pet.

[H]OW TO CHOOSE A KITTEN OR
[CA]T

[I]n selecting a suitable
[kit]ten or cat, there are two
[asp]ects that are likely to be
[im]portant. In the case of the
[po]tential breeder/exhibitor,
[you] will want a quality kitten.
[Th]e reality is that you cannot
[be] advised of such selection
[fro]m a book. You must do

When selecting a kitten, it does
not matter which sex it is. Either
sex can make a loving and
affectionate pet.

some background research
and locate a breeder of reputation. This done, you can do
no more than place your trust
in such a person to guide you
in your selection. In most
instances, you will get what
you pay for: so don't expect to
get a show stopper at a pet
price—it never happens.

Another consideration is in
regard to the health of the
kitten, or cat, irrespective of
its quality. You will appreciate
that the purchase of any
living creature, especially a
young one, carries with it a
degree of risk, so it is a case
of reducing this to its most

acceptable level. There is no
one source that is guaranteed
to sell you a cat that will
survive, but some sources are
more risky than others. First,
however, we will look at key
points to note when you
inspect kittens and cats.

1. Begin by watching which
   kittens seem the most
   outgoing. These are your
   best choice. The timid
   kitten that is afraid to
   approach you is likely to
   turn out very nervous—it
   may also be more prone
   to illness.

2. Notice the kittens at play
   and watch for those that
   show signs of a disability
   in their movements. They
   may only be suffering
   from a rough-and-tumble
   strain, or they may have
   an impediment to their

limbs. Rule out any that display a problem.

3. Now you can make a physical examination of the kitten. Begin with the head.

The *eyes* should be round and bright with no signs of weeping. A cat has what is called a haw, or third eyelid. It is the nictitating membrane and is seen in the lower corner of the eye. If it is raised over part of the eye, this invariably indicates a problem—slight though this may be. However, it could be serious, so if seen this would mean a rejection. The *nose* should be dry with no signs of congealed mucus. Open the kitten's *mouth* and smell its breath. The odor should not be unpleasant. The *teeth* will be small and white with no

build up of tartar on them in a kitten. They should be either a level bite (the incisors of the upper jaw just touching those of the lower jaw), or they will be a scissor, or pincer, bite (the upper incisors just overlapping the lower ones). An undershot jaw (lower incisors protruding in front of those of the upper jaw) is undesirable but is seen in some breeds. The *ears* will be erect, well furred, and with no visible abrasions. They should be sweet smelling. Brown wax in the ears is a

---

The considerably long life span of cats—around 15 to 20 years or so—means that you can have a goodly number of years to enjoy your feline friend.

---

sign of parasitic activity. It not a major problem if it is promptly attended to, but i not a good sign. The *fur* of a kitten will not be quite as profuse as in the adult, but will look healthy. It should smell pleasant. Part the fur inspect for parasites. Small blackish-red specks indicat flea dirt, so look further— behind the ears and at the base of the tail. Fleas are ve mobile, whereas lice are gra and slow moving. They indi cate poor living conditions. Any bald areas indicate a problem, especially if they a in the form of whorls, whicl are the result of fungal atta The *abdomen* should be we filled without being pot bel- lied, which might suggest worm infestation. It should free of abrasions. *Feet*: The

Top: Red classic tabby and white longhaired American Curls. Bottom: Selkirk Rex kittens. A healthy kitten will be bright eyed, alert, and in full coat. When selecting a kitten, health should be your primary consideration.

…ould be five toes on the …ont feet and four toes on the …nd feet. Each toe should …ve a claw. The pads on the …ws should be soft in a …tten but harder in an adult. …metimes a cat may have six …es, termed polydactyly. This …not a problem in a pet cat …t is a no-no in an exhibition …breeding animal. Declawed …ts are ineligible for exhibi- …n under nearly all registra- …n body rules. The *tail* …ould ideally be kink free in …exhibition or breeding cat. …nks are more likely to be …nd in foreign breeds. …You may not have the …portunity of seeing the fecal …atter of a kitten or cat, but if …u do, it should be firm and …t liquid. Any blood streaks …it are a clear sign of an internal disorder. It should be added that the bowel movements of kittens are much more changeable than those of the adult. This being so, a change in diet, a slight cold, in fact many causes can result in the feces of a kitten becoming rather more liquid, but they should never be like water.

If you are selecting an adult cat, you must make sure it can be handled. Take due caution when lifting it up; an adult can inflict serious damage to your face with its claws. Some cats that are otherwise quite friendly do not take kindly to strangers suddenly lifting them up. If the cat is clearly of an aggressive nature, do not select it

regardless of how attractive it is—this applies doubly so if you have children in your home.

WHERE TO OBTAIN A KITTEN OR CAT

The answer to this question will be dependent on why the cat is being purchased. For a quality exhibition or breeding feline, you must obviously seek out a suitable breeder — preferably in your locality, so that you can become friends with them. You may wish to

Persian. If you have your heart set on this very popular breed of cat, remember that you will have to regularly devote time to a grooming regimen.

acquire more of their stock as you become established. Do not purchase a show cat from a breeder solely because the breeder is local; such a person must have a good reputation. Make inquiries at local shows and via your vet. Time spent in research is rarely wasted: it could save you a great deal of future costs.

For the potential pet owner naturally the pet shop is the first source that comes to mind. Be sure that a kitten sold in a store is already vaccinated against the major feline diseases and you should be just fine.

Finally, have your vet give the kitten a thorough physical checkup—regardless of the source.

Breeds such as the Himalayan are the embodiment of grace and beauty. They add a touch of class to any household.

feeding

A Javanese queen meticulously grooming her youngster. In essence, Javanese are longhaired Colorpoint Shorthairs.

FEEDING

Feeding your cat or kitten basically very simple, given number of commercial cat ods now available. As long you have a good can ener and a modicum of eful information, you are in siness—it really is that sy. The essential information in regard to feline feeding as follows:

The cat is a prime carnivore, so its diet must reflect this fact. It should contain a goodly percentage of protein in the form of meat, poultry, or fish.
All food given to cats should be fresh. Apart from the fact that well-cared-for cats will turn their nose up at most foods that are not fresh, there is the obvious danger to them of becoming ill from bacteria in stale or "off" food. If you don't like the look or smell of a food item, the simple rule is to trash it. Try to give your kitten plenty of variety when it is young. This reduces (though does not eliminate) the likelihood of it becoming a faddy eater when it matures. Apart from this, the wider the variety the less likely it

will be that an important ingredient is missing. The reality of feeding cats is that if you feed them on the best brands of canned foods and dry kibble, they will refuse the cheaper brands. Most of us spoil our cats, so if they are brought up on quality brands, be sure you at

With the wide variety of commercial cat foods that are on the market today, there is no reason for your cat to have a boring diet. Your vet can suggest a feeding program that is right for your cat.

least vary these between the beef, poultry, and fish offerings. Be warned that too much fish food is not good for your kitty: many cats will return this shortly afterward—via vomiting!

4. Avoid feeding food that contains fine bones. Cats enjoy meat on the bone; it

is the splinter types that should be avoided.

5. If fresh meat is given, it must be of a standard fit for human consumption.

6. Do not try to trim the food bill by giving your cat the brands prepared for dogs. These contain a higher percentage of carbohydrates and not enough protein for a cat. This is why they are less expensive in the first place.

WHEN TO FEED AND HOW MUCH

Cats should be fed little and often, whenever this is convenient to your daily routine. The actual feeding times are not important at all, but they should be regular once times have been established. Some people feed twice a day, some three. In our household, we are at home all day so the cats are fed on an ad lib basis throughout the day. This means certain of them will get maybe three feeds, others as many as five to seven, depending on the cat in question. All cats differ in the amount they will eat: some are small eaters, while others are little piggies.

The amount to feed is linked to how often you are feeding and the quality of the food. If your cats get a number of meals, they will clearly eat smaller amounts than if they only have two or three meals a day. A high-protein content food will satiate the cat more readily than will a dish full of rice, bits of vegetable leftovers, and a few scraps of meat. The two basic guides as to whether or not you are feeding your cat well enough are:

1. Does it look well muscled and exhibit a gorgeous-looking sleek coat?
2. Does it walk away from its dish in a satisfied manner or is it licking up every last bit and clearly wanting more? In the latter instance, it probably is not getting enough. If it leaves some food on its plate at every meal, and if the quality of the food is good, then you can reduce the quantity. You will establish the right amount on a trial and error basis.

FEEDING KITTENS

There are special brands of kitten food available if you want them. When feeding dry cat food, you must be sure the pieces are small enough for the kitten to crunch. Kittens have small and rather weak teeth, so they cannot cope with kibbled food too well until they are about ten or more weeks of age. You can provide dried cat food on an ad lib basis, so the kitten and adults can have it whenever they wish. You will find that some cats prefer dried food while others partake of a few kibbles only every so often.

Water should always be available to your kitten and cats, even if they drink very little of it. This is more likely if

their basic diet is of moist canned food, which contains a high percentage of water. A young kitten should receive four or more meals per day.

A kitten should be fed four or more times per day, and the food should contain small pieces that are easy for smaller mouths to chew. Dry food that is sold especially for kittens may be a good choice.

COMMERCIAL FOOD

Apart from food specially packaged or canned for cats, there are many kitchen items that your kitten or cat will enjoy. These should be chopped up into pieces that are small enough for your pet to cope with.

Fresh meat: Cut up a few pieces from the meat you are having. For kittens, it must be scraped or minced into very small pieces. Liver is rich in vitamins, but much is lost during cooking. Do not supply too much liver; otherwise, the kitten or cat will have a stomach upset.

Fish: These are rich in proteins and essential amino acids. They are best steamed or grilled. Sardines and other fish canned in oils will be greatly enjoyed periodically and are rich in vitamins. Do not overfeed canned fish as it will prove too rich for young kittens.

Eggs: This food is rich in protein. Serve boiled and chopped.

Cheese: This is rich in protein and greatly enjoyed in small amounts by most cats. It can be served as is or cooked with other food.

Carbohydrates: Examples are bread, pasta, rice, and unsweetened breakfast cereals. Some cats will tolerate a small amount of carbohydrates mixed with meat;

Treats can be provided on an occasional basis to help provide a little variety in the diet. Some treats act as a cleansing agent to help reduce tartar on the cat's teeth. Photo courtesy of Heinz.

feeding

...ers will all but ignore such ...d. This will depend on how ...ll fed they are. Carbohy- ...ates are not essential food ...ms for cats but are in- ...uded in commercial diets to ...ovide bulk and to keep the ...st down. They are the ...eapest and most readily ...ailable source of energy food, ...t are of no value in terms of

building muscle tissue.

Fruit and vegetables: In the wild, these are supplied via the stomach contents of the cat's prey. In such, they are partially digested and thus can be assimilated in the cat's body. A cat cannot utilize raw vegetable matter, so it must be boiled first so that the tough cellulose walls

are broken down. Small amounts of vegetables and fruits can be mixed in with freshly cooked meats.

Sweet Items: Cats do not have a sweet tooth as do dogs so are rarely interested in items such as cakes or sweet cookies. This is just as well as these items are not good for their teeth.

Right: In addition to their food, cats should have access to fresh water at all times. Do not give your cat milk, as it can cause digestive problems. Bottom: Dry kibbled food can be provided on an ad lib basis; canned food should not be left out for any great length of time because it can spoil.

GENERAL CARE

Cats are no problem at all to cater to in their day-to-day management, but when a kitten is arriving into your home, you should be aware of potential dangers. Adult cats are very cautious creatures, but kittens are adventurous and learn about dangers only as they mature. You must therefore think for them.

1. Do not leave irons and other electrical appliances plugged into sockets. A kitten may try to climb the cords or bite into them.

2. Be sure that any balconies are screened so that the kitten is in no danger of falling off.

3. Be sure that washing and drying machine doors are always closed because kittens have been known to clamber in and then decide to take a nap! Fish tanks should be fitted with canopies so that the kitten is in no danger of falling into them. Open fireplaces must be protected with a suitable mesh guard.

6. Houseplants should be well out of reach of the kitten, as some are poisonous.

7. Trash cans should be secured so that the kitten cannot rummage through them. They may contain dangerous items, such as

the sharp edges of food cans, which the kitten might lick.

8. Young children should never be left alone with kittens. They do not understand how delicate these are. This also applies to a dog if you

Your feline friend will reap the benefits of proper nutrition: healthy skin and coat, bright eyes, plenty of energy, and all-around good health. Photo courtesy of Nutro. Call (800)833-5330 for the pet dealer nearest you.

have one. They are only safe together once they are well acquainted.

9. Cherished items, such as ornaments, are best placed well out of reach of a kitten, which might easily knock them from low shelves it might clamber onto.

A KITTEN'S FIRST DAYS IN YOU HOME

When it is time to pick up your kitten, try to do this early in the day so the kitten has plenty of time to settle into its new home.

Be sure to ask the seller what feeding regimen the kitten is familiar with. Stick to this for a week and then gradually make any desired changes. This will remove the risk of an upset stomach due to the sudden upheaval i the kitten's life. You will also need the kitten's vaccination certificates, and its pedigree and registration transfer forms if these are applicable.

If the journey home is a long one, take the carry box, or a cut-down cardboard box, lined with toweling for the kitten to sleep on. It may be sick so be prepared for this. Have water and maybe some dry cat food with you, and make periodic stops so its stomach has a few minutes rest from the vehicle's momentum, which it will not be used to. It would be wise to also take a litter tray, complete with some litter, on long journeys. Once back at home you can start by letting the kitten explore the kitchen. It might appreciate some water and may even be hungry. It may also wish to have a sleep Do not let children pester it. I will urinate very soon after it has drank, been to sleep, or

n playing, and will want to
ecate shortly after eating.
litter tray should be placed
a convenient location.
f the kitten has not been
ccinated, or if the vaccina-
ns are not yet effective
out four weeks from date
en), do not let the kitten
t of doors. When it is
ltime, place the kitten in
carry box, bed, or wherever
s to sleep. By all
ans supply a cuddly
if you have only the
e kitten, and this
l in some way offset
fact that it no
ger has its litter-
tes to curl up next
You may decide to
it sleep on your
d, but if this is to be
ne you should not
ange your mind as
e kitten grows up.

TER TRAINING
A kitten cannot
ntrol its bowels for
ry long so you must
watchful at certain
es as already mentioned.
e kitten will begin to cry
d will start to look around
a secluded spot in which
attend its toiletry needs.
en you see it doing this,
u must act promptly and
ace the kitten in its litter
y.
Gently hold its paws and
ratch them into the litter. It
ll usually oblige. If not, and
jumps out of the tray, you
ust continue to watch it and
peat the operation. It will
ry quickly catch on as to
at is required. You must,
wever, accept that the odd
cident will happen. The tray
ust be kept clean; other-
se, the kitten will not be
couraged to use it.

SCRATCHING POST TRAINING
This is done in much the
same manner as litter training. When you see the kitten
start to claw at the carpet or
the furniture, quickly lift it up
and take it to the scratching
post. You can draw its paws
down the post and, once
again, after a few lessons it
will understand it is allowed
to scratch this, but not the

It's important to keep your cat's litter box clean, and a variety of litters is available to make your job easier. Photo courtesy of Swheat Scoop/Pet Care Systems, Inc. Call (800)SWEATS for the pet dealer nearest you.

furniture. As it gets older you
can say "no" in a firm voice if
it goes to scratch anything.
You can also give it a light tap
on its hindquarters—providing
you can actually catch it in the
act. Such discipline will be
meaningless if it is given even
a few seconds after the kitten
has committed a misde-
meanor. Always remember that
cats, like dogs, relate only to
the present, not to the past.

LEAD TRAINING
Cats are not happy on a
lead even though some will
tolerate one if trained from a
young age. They feel very
exposed and vulnerable when
constrained. If they are
startled by something, they
will immediately struggle to
free themselves, and will then
panic and run off. If they are
in a strange environment, you
may lose your pet. I
would therefore not
recommend the average
pet owner to attempt
lead training their cat.
Cats of foreign type
usually respond better
to lead training than do
other breeds. If you do
decide to train your cat
to walk on a lead, never
attempt to drag it. Let it
go where it wants, then
slowly, once it is famil-
iar with the restraint of
a lead, you can gently
persuade it to travel in
the direction that you
wish. Fit the cat with a
harness so that you
have more control over it
should it suddenly panic.

GROOMING
Grooming a shorthaired cat
is simplicity itself. However, it
should be done on a regular
basis, both in order that the
cat becomes used to being
handled, and so you can take
the opportunity to give it a
physical check. Use the brush
to groom with the lie of the
hair, commencing on its neck.
When the brushing is com-
pleted, you can then use the
fine comb and repeat the
operation. Take care when
combing its underbelly as this
is more sensitive. Finish with
a silk or chamois leather to
give the coat a nice shine.

Examine the cat's ears, teeth, and fur for any signs of parasites. Longhaired cats need grooming daily. Commence with a brisk brushing with the lie of the fur, then brush against it, and finally back with the lie. This should remove tangles and most debris that may be clinging to it. Next you can use the wide- or medium-toothed comb to groom with the lie—then against it. Should you feel any stiff resistance, find the offending tangle and tease it out with your fingers. At all times you must be as gentle as possible; otherwise, the cat will soon come to dislike being groomed. You can end by using the fine-toothed comb, and by using a stiff toothbrush on the fur of the face.

If the cat should get dirty, which is unusual for cats, you can clean it by sprinkling talcum powder or powdered chalk into the fur, then thoroughly groom it out. Be sure it is well groomed out as longhaired cats always spend much time licking their fur. If you decide the cat needs a bath, be very sure that longhaired cats are extremely well groomed prior to the bath; otherwise the fur will become badly matted, and you will find it very difficult to groom out the tangles. When bathing, take great care that no water enters its eyes, as this will make a difficult task even more so. It will usually be helpful if someone assists you with the bathing—one to hold the cat and one to attend to the actual washing.

The shampoo must be thoroughly rinsed out of the fur; otherwise, it will make it sticky and could cause an irritation. Be sure the water is only lukewarm, and ensure that the cat is not allowed out of doors until it is thoroughly dry.

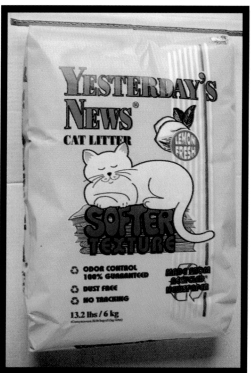

Cat litter has come a long way since the days of dried clay! Today's litters are dust-free, super-absorbent and don't get stuck in kitty's paws. Photo courtesy of Yesterday's News®.

HANDLING KITTENS AND CATS

Never lift a kitten or cat up by the scruff of its neck: this is quite incorrect. It should always be supported under its chest with one hand while being secured to your chest with the other.

Children must be taught to handle a kitten with great respect because, from an early age, even a kitten can inflict a very nasty scratch to a child's face or arms if it is handled in other than a gentle manner. Some cats will allow you to cradle them baby fashion on their backs; others will resent this and struggle to get free. Never insist that the pet cat be held in an unnatural position. The show cat must be handled very often from a young age so that it shows no resentment of this—or by being raised at arms length by a stranger: this is how the judge will inspect the exhibit.

If you find that your cat does become aggressive when being handled and if you must place it into its carry box in order to transport it to the vet or elsewhere, be sure you have a good hold of its two front legs—behind the elbow. Next, secure a firm hold of the rear legs; otherwise, these will quickly rake your arm.

Alternatively, place a towel over the cat's body, which will reduce its ability to scratch you. If you have handled a cat from the time it was a kitten, you should not have problems; but adopted adults may be a different matter, even though they are otherwise friendly. They may not like being placed into a carry box for example.

TRAVELING WITH CATS

Like people and dogs, some cats travel well in cars; others never take to it. Even good traveling cats may initially

Now what do I do?!!!

start to howl, or be sick, but thereafter they settle down without further problem. Never allow the cat to be loose in a car if you are the sole occupant. Do not give travel sickness pills without your vet's advice. The vet may be able to supply a better sedative if this is needed. Never leave your cat in a vehicle on hot days. The cat could die from heat exhaustion. If a cat is clearly suffering from heat stroke, you must bring its body temperature down as rapidly as possible. Soak it in a wet towel, or dunk it into a tub of cool water (but not its head, which can be wiped with a cold piece of cloth).

TRAVELING ABROAD

When a cat is transported by air or sea, it must be placed into a secure container, such as a carry box. Airlines and shippers may differ in the exact requirements of a container, so you are advised to check this out well in advance of any such journey.

You should also check with the country of destination what regulations they may have in regard to importing cats into their country. For example, all livestock entering Great Britain, Australia, New Zealand, Hawaii, and certain other countries, must go through a six-month quarantine period. Cats are not required at this time to go into quarantine when entering the US, but must have satisfactory veterinary health certificates. The same is generally true when entering mainland European countries, which may additionally require proof of vaccination against rabies. Regulations can change at any time, so reference to old

literature may be out of date. Your veterinarian will be able to help you in finding out the current regulations.

VACATIONS

In general, cats do not enjoy accompanying you on vacation. They are territorial creatures, and so would rather remain in the familiar environment of their own home. This so, when you go away try to arrange for a relative or friend to call in each day and feed your cat, and maybe spend a few minutes with it. This is preferable to placing it in a cattery that boards felines. If you do board your cat, inspect the boarding establishment first so that you are satisfied that they have a competent staff and adequate accommodations. A veterinary recommendation is preferred. Any worthwhile cattery will insist on seeing current certificates of vaccination against the major feline diseases.

INTRODUCING CATS TO OTHER PETS

If you already have a cat, a dog, or a large parrot, the introduction of a kitten or cat may go smoothly, or may present problems, depending on the temperament of the resident pets and the newcomer. Kittens are generally less difficult to introduce because they are not aware that they may not be appreciated by the other pets. They simply want to make friends. An adopted adult cat, on the other hand, may have had a bad experience with other animals, so it may be less charitable about making friends. Other cats will be curious about the newcomer,

who will approach them wit caution. They will probably sniff the kitten, hiss at it, a move away. They may even box its ears a few times. However, they are aware tha it is a baby of their own kin so will normally just ignore initially. As the days go by, they will get used to it. Som adults will become a sort of aunt or uncle to the kitten and will soon be playing wit it. Others will eventually accept it without ever gettin on really friendly terms.

When an adult cat is introduced to a home with a resident feline, the newcome may be accepted without problem, or the fur may sta to fly. There is nothing you can do to make cats be friendly with each other or other pets. They must sort their relationships out between themselves.

If a dog is the other pet, only you know its nature. Y must beware that it does no attack the kitten. Even if it i known to chase cats, it may well accept the kitten—give time. Some will play happily with cats; others treat them with quiet indifference. Neve hold a kitten in front of another pet, as this is court ing disaster.

Large parrots usually ignore kittens after they ha had time to study them. Mc kittens, and indeed cats, wi not wish to press their atte tions on any large parrot th is equipped with a raucous voice and a powerful beak. should go without saying, until you are very sure of h the kitten or cat is being accepted by other non-cat residents, you should neve leave them alone together when you are not present.

Young children must be taught to handle a kitten with great respect because, from an early age, even a kitten can inflict a nasty scratch if it is handled roughly.

HEALTH

Although you might think that disease has little merit, it is in fact a vital part of survival. It ensures that only the fittest live to perpetuate their species. It is a regulator that thins down excessive numbers in the wild habitat. It is thus an essential part of the complex web of life. This said, none of us want to see our cherished pets die, or even suffer, because of an illness.

The ways that we can prevent this from happening are threefold:

1. By ensuring that our cats are well fed and well managed.
2. By recognizing the signs of ill health.
3. By ensuring that we take prompt action to arrest disease or ill health should they occur.

The first course of action has been covered in earlier chapters, so here we can review numbers 2 and 3.

RECOGNIZING ILL HEALTH

A cat cannot tell us when it feels ill, so the only way we can know is by observation. This will reveal an illness in one of two ways. Either the cat will display clinical signs of a problem, or its behavior will not be normal. To appreciate the latter, we must be aware of what normality is for the cat in question. The greedy eater may suddenly show lack of interest in its food. The energetic cat will be less so. All ill cats will tend to seek quiet spots where they can lay down and sleep.

Clinical signs of ill health are any or all of the following:

1. A discharge from the eyes or nose.
2. Dull eyes, with the haw becoming very visible.
3. Dull and staring coat. A very dry coat.
4. A cat that constantly coughs or makes a wheezing sound when breathing. All cats cough now and again, but this is different from the continual coughing of the ill cat.

5. Vomiting. Cats will often vomit after eating grass (which acts as a natural purgative), eating a food that is too rich for their stomach, or simply because they have eaten too much (greedy feede⎖ This is totally different from the cat that is repeatedly sick, especi⎖ a few times during any 24-hour period.
6. If the cat scratches a great deal, this too wou⎖ indicate a problem—su⎖ as parasites. Yet again, must be appreciated th⎖ all cats like a good scratch every so often.
7. The bowel movements ⎖ a cat are normally reasonably firm in texture. so if they become loose this would suggest a minor tummy upset or the first signs of something more serious. If they became more liquid, and maybe streaked with blood, t⎖ would definitely be abnormal.
8. If a cat suddenly starts lose weight, something amiss.
9. If a cat suddenly starts drink a lot of water, yet its diet has not change⎖ then there is a problem⎖

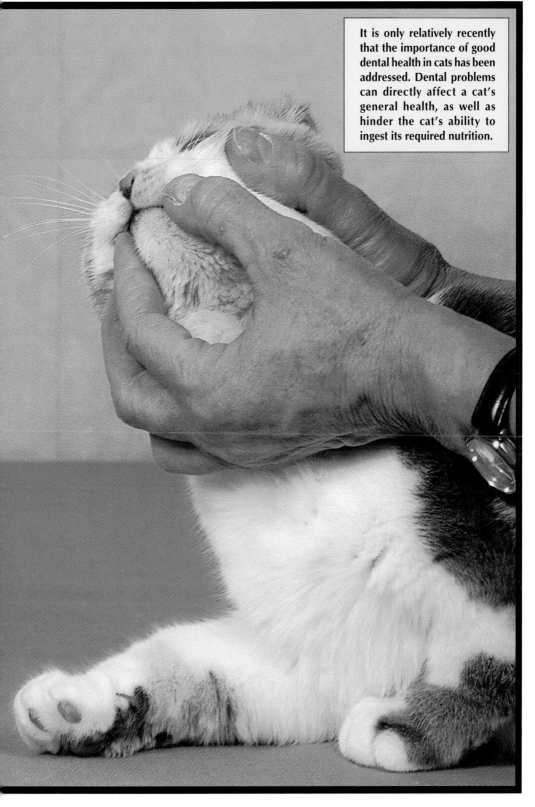

It is only relatively recently that the importance of good dental health in cats has been addressed. Dental problems can directly affect a cat's general health, as well as hinder the cat's ability to ingest its required nutrition.

34

health

> **Pet dental products are available for helping to fight plaque, reduce tartar build-up, and control unpleasant breath. Photo courtesy of Four Paws.**

(assuming it is not just a case of the weather being unusually hot).

10. Bleeding. Any cat that bleeds from the mouth, the anus, the vulva, or the penis clearly has something wrong with it.

11. Impediment to its movement, or any other obvious anatomical problem.

There are a considerable number of diseases that a cat can suffer from, but only a limited number of ways that such problems can show themselves. This means that many of the clinical signs can cover a number of diseases. There is no way that an unqualified person can diagnose the problem —thus the treatment. This means that you must consult a veterinarian for all but the most minor of problems, and even they are not without risk. The problem may indeed be of a minor nature, but it may also be the beginning of a serious disease. How are you to tell? If you are wrong, the disease has had more time to become

advanced, and it already had a head start before you noticed clinical signs.

If two or more of the signs noted above are being displayed by the cat, you need to consult your vet right away. If bleeding of any kind (other than from a minor cut) occurs, you must again consult your vet. If a supposedly minor condition does not improve within 24-48 hours, it is not minor.

TAKING PROMPT ACTION

For the vast majority of conditions, you should promptly call your vet. You should have first written down the clinical signs so that you do not forget anything. The vet will probably ask you about the cat's diet, state of its bowel movements, when it was last ill, if its vaccinations

are up to date, and if anyth[ing] in the cat's environment ha[s] changed recently. Based on this discussion, the vet will then suggest a course of action, which would norma[lly] be to visit the clinic so that [it] can give the cat a complete physical examination.

If the cat is suffering from parasitic infestation, such a[s] lice or fleas, you must eradi[-] cate these quickly by using one of the modern remedies from your pet shop or veter[i-] narian. They are usually effective against most common parasites. Fleas and mites leave the host for periods of time in order to la[y] eggs—lice spend their life cycle on the host. It is thus important that the bedding [of] a cat is thoroughly treated; otherwise, reinfestation will occur after treating the cat. [It] is best to burn blanketing after severe attacks.

Cuts: Minor cuts should [be] wiped clean with a mild antiseptic solution. Antisep[tic] ointment can be smeared o[n] the wound, but usually the cat will lick it off. For more serious cuts, the flow of blo[od] should be stemmed by appl[y-] ing a lint and bandage, afte[r] first cleaning the wound. B[e] sure bandages are not too tight. Rush the cat to the ve[t].

Burns: These are of two kinds: chemical and direct heat. If the former, wash the skin by using plenty of wate[r]. If the burn is from direct hea[t] cool the site with water or a[n] ice pack, then apply a thin f[ilm] of an antibiotic. In both instances, consult the vet, who may need to treat the cat for shock. In severe cases, take emergency action as describ[ed] then wrap the cat in a blank[et] and rush it to the nearest ve[t]

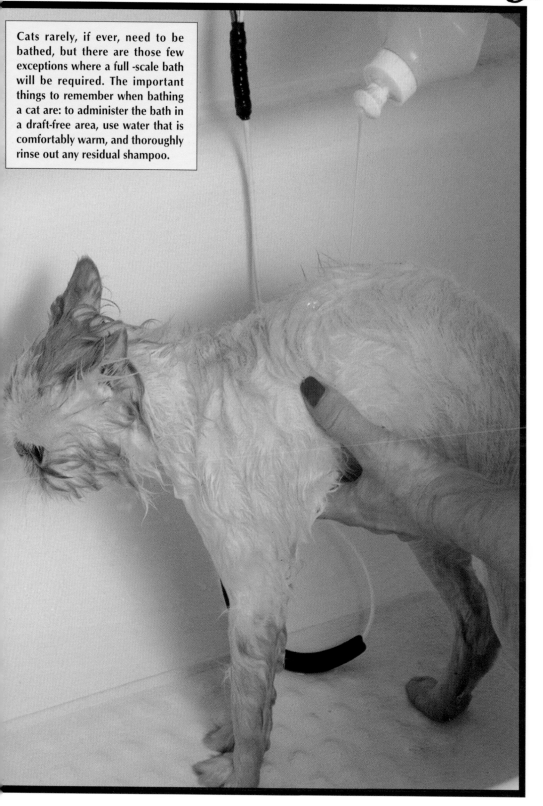

Cats rarely, if ever, need to be bathed, but there are those few exceptions where a full-scale bath will be required. The important things to remember when bathing a cat are: to administer the bath in a draft-free area, use water that is comfortably warm, and thoroughly rinse out any residual shampoo.

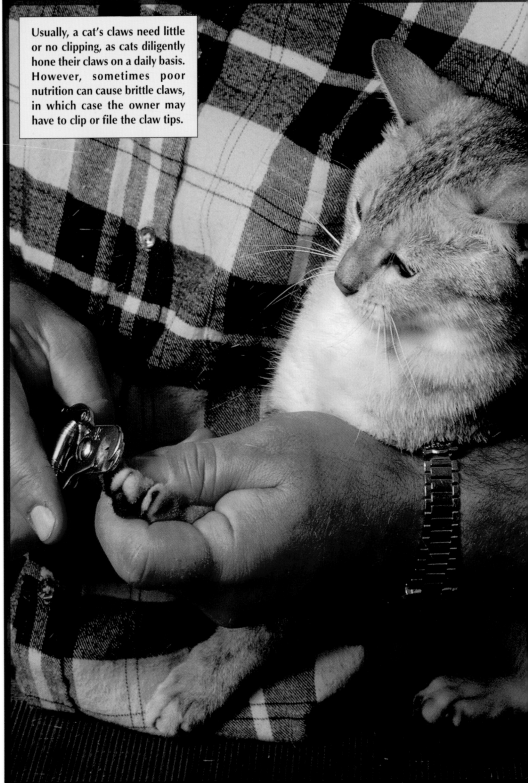

Usually, a cat's claws need little or no clipping, as cats diligently hone their claws on a daily basis. However, sometimes poor nutrition can cause brittle claws, in which case the owner may have to clip or file the claw tips.

Accidents: The course of [acti]on is to first move the cat [to a] safe place. Try to place a [bla]nket or even a piece of [car]dboard under the cat so it [can] be moved. Avoid lifting its [hea]d to prevent blood from [trac]king up into the throat [and] possibly blocking the [air] passages. Place a [bla]nket over the cat to keep [it w]arm, then either rush [the] cat to the vet or await [its] arrival, talking in a [soo]thing manner to the cat. [If s]hock is likely, place the [cat] in a darkened room if [pos]sible.

[VA]CCINATIONS & MAJOR [DIS]EASES

[T]he respiratory and [inte]stinal tracts, together [with] the heart, are three [sou]rces of major killer [dise]ases in cats. You can [prot]ect the cat against [som]e of them with vaccina[tion]s. You should contact [you]r vet as soon as a kitten [or c]at is acquired if it has [not] already been vacci[nat]ed. Booster shots are [requ]ired annually to ensure [con]tinued protection.

[F]eline influenza: This is [cau]sed by numerous [viru]ses (microscopic bacte[ria).]It is normally trans[mitt]ed by direct contact from [one] cat to another, or by the [cat] being in a place where an [infe]cted cat has been. High [risk] areas are catteries, cat [sho]ws, and veterinary clinics. [Prot]ection is via a vaccination [give]n when the kitten is eight [or m]ore weeks of age. A [boo]ster is given about 21 days [late]r, and the kitten is not [full]y protected until seven [day]s after the booster.

[F]eline enteritis [(pan]leucopenia): This is

another viral disease, transmitted by direct/indirect contact or by a vector such as a flea. It is highly contagious but can be protected against by a vaccination given at the same time as that for cat flu.

Feline leukemia virus (FeLV): This dreaded disease

may show itself in a variety of ways, including anemia, vomiting, tumors, and acute diarrhea. Cats may become immune to it, but many die. It is highly contagious and spreads by direct contact with other cats. There is now a vaccination that helps protect cats against this disease. Your vet can test a cat for the virus. This is suggested when purchasing any costly feline. A certificate indicating that the kitten or cat is FeLV negative will then be supplied. It is advisable to insist on seeing a certificate when sending a queen to be mated.

VETERINARY TREATMENTS

When you are given tablets or liquids with which to dose your kitten or cat, it is essential that you follow the vet's instructions to the letter. Do not stop the treatment just because the cat appears to have made a dramatic recovery. This could result in a relapse and may also result in bacteria developing immunity against the medications given. Your vet will often supply vitamin pills when a treatment has been given. This is because medicines may not be selective in the bacteria they kill, meaning beneficial ones are also destroyed. These may include those responsible for the synthesis of certain vitamins, which will have been supplied orally pending the recolonization of the digestive tract with the needed organisms.

It only takes a minute for your cat or kitten to get lost—and yet it only takes a minute or so to get an I.D. tag that will protect your cat from being lost permanently. Protect your pet with the most visible identification system available: a tag. Photo courtesy of Quick Tag; for the location of the Quick Tag™ Engraving System machine nearest you, call 1-888-600-TAGS.

CAT BREEDS

The number of cat breeds that you can choose from will be between 35-50, depending on the country you live in and which cats are accepted as breeds by the differing registration authorities. However, the number of breeds in the UK is greatly in excess of 50 because, in the case of the Persian, for example, every color is regarded as a breed. In the US, the breed is Persian, and the colors are simply varieties of it. A brief discussion of the way domestic cats are classified will perhaps be both interesting and helpful to the newcomer to purebred cats, who is sometimes rather mystified by the apparent complexity of the subject.

DOMESTIC CAT CLASSIFICATION

The most basic division of the breeds is into groups based on coat length. There are thus longhairs and shorthairs. The longhairs comprise two quite distinct types. There are those of Persian origin, which have

> **European Shorthair. Some fanciers claim that this breed goes back to the days of the Roman Empire. This sturdy, medium-to-large breed is a very popular European house cat.**

profuse coats, and those of foreign origin. This latter term is used to describe the physical type. In essence, they have the conformation of a Siamese cat whereas the Persian is a more stocky and solidly built feline. The shorthairs are likewise divisible into the European types, with cobby powerful bodies and round heads, and the foreigns. The latter, again, are most readily appreciated being of the Siamese type—from which a number were developed. They have lithe bodies and a wedge-shaped head. Cats thus have three main basic ancestral stocks, with two subdivisions:

American Shorthair, silver patched tabby. As American as apple pie, this hardy breed served as chief mouser for the pilgrims when they were establishing themselves in their new land.

European Shorthairs of stocky type. The coat is thick, glossy, and short. Persian cats. These have dense woolly fur, but originally there were two types: those with woolly fur and those with a much more silky texture. The latter are today exemplified by the Turkish breeds.

The foreigns. These are very slim, generally long-legged breeds. The Siamese is the best known example. Other foreigns are of Siamese type but more stocky and with rounder faces. By interbreeding with these sic stocks, all present-day

Siamese queen and her kitten. Siamese cats are said to be the closest thing to a dog in a cat. They are known for their affectionate and attentive nature.

Top: Cymric. A longhaired version of the Manx, examples of this breed first appeared in Canada in the mid-1960s. The body is tailless and round, with a broad chest. The breed is available in a variety of colors and combinations of colors. Bottom: Persian, red tabby. This striking breed of cat is the most popular breed in the US. It is distinguished by its long, flowing coat and large, prominent eyes.

domestic cats have been produced. When a major mutation is transferred fro[m] one breed to another, or if [it] an independent or new mut[a]tion, this will result in a ne[w] breed. For example, a longhaired Siamese is calle[d] Balinese, while a longhaire[d] Abyssinian is a Somali. Wh[en] the Persian was crossed wi[th] the Siamese, the result be-came known as a Himalaya[n]. This latter breed is now regarded as purely a color variant of the Persian in m[ost] US registrations. In Great Britain, the Himalayan of t[he] US would be regarded as a Colourpoint Longhair. Whe[n] the American Shorthair is crossed with the Burmese, [the] resulting cat is called a Bombay. New breeds are constantly in the making. I[n] order to be accepted as suc[h]

cat breeds

...ey must fulfill certain
...iteria as laid down by the
...rious cat registration
...sociations. Some of the
...ter (for example, the Cat
...nciers' Association in the
...S, and the Governing
...uncil of the Cat Fancy in
...reat Britain), are very
...rticular about breed
...alification. Others are less
...rict, which is why there are
...us a variable number of
...cognized breeds. However,
...ost of the long-established
...eeds are recognized by all
...gistrations, including the
...mous Manx cat. This breed
...uld not be accepted by a
...umber of registrations were
...not for its long establish-
...ent. It is based on a
...netic abnormality that
...any associations today
...uld outlaw.

Balinese. This breed is available in the same colors as in the Siamese. Balinese are slender, lithe cats with long plumy tails. In temperament, they are gentle and affectionate.

Birman, also known as the Sacred Cat of Burma. Each of the four colorpoints (seal, chocolate, blue, and lilac) of this breed are accentuated by pure white "gloves." Legend has it that Birmans were the sacred cats kept long ago in the Buddhist temples of Burma.

42

American Shorthair enjoying a meal. Its well-defined tabby pattern is seen in a number of other breeds.

COLORS AND PATTERNS

There are about twenty possible colors to be seen in cats, and they may have differing names in various countries. This can give the impression that there are substantially more colors than there actually are. From a genetic viewpoint, there are probably less than 16 colors, but they can range in shade as a result of breeder selection for lighter or darker tones. The same color may be given a different name from one country to another, so the chocolate of the UK is the champagne of the US. Further, a color term may be applied specifically to a given breed, so the sable of the Burmese would normally be called seal in most other breeds of Siamese origin. These differences, when crossing international borders, can make life difficult for the novice.

The patterns seen in cat coats are basically the following:

1. **Tabby patterns:** These may be mackerel (which is the wild type), blotched, or classic (which is the more popular type).
2. **Spots:** This pattern has gained considerably in popularity and is a feature of a number of the newer breeds now being established. It is not known for sure whether spotted patterns are independent patterns or the result of the break up of tabby stripes.
3. **Pointed (Siamese):** This pattern is known as Himalayan in most other pet animals. The extremities of the coat (face, ears, paws, and tail) are a darker shade than that of the body. This pattern is thermosensitive in that the points become paler as the temperature increases.
4. **Composites:** These are when two differing elements are combined. The bicolor, such as black and white, the tortoiseshell (and white), the cameos, and the blue-cream, are but a few of the vast number of potential composites.

Siamese, six-month-old seal point. The pointed pattern is thermosensitive: the points become paler as the temperature increases.

cat breeds

When the various colors are ~~p~~ermuted with the coat ~~pa~~tterns, the result is an ~~in~~credible list of possibilities. ~~In~~ certain breeds, the color is ~~a v~~ital part of the breed. The ~~Ko~~rat, for example, is a blue ~~ca~~t. In most breeds, however, ~~th~~e color is not so significant ~~in~~ determining breed status, ~~th~~erefore you can obtain the ~~br~~eed in whatever color ~~va~~rieties have been estab-~~lis~~hed at this time. In general, ~~on~~ce a breed is established, it ~~wi~~ll be found that colors are ~~oft~~en added to it.

When new colors are ~~ad~~ded, they may result in a ~~ne~~w breed name being applied ~~be~~cause in some breeds, such ~~as~~ the Siamese, the number of ~~ac~~cepted colors is often ~~lim~~ited by a given registration ~~au~~thority. Self-colored ~~Si~~amese, for example, are ~~kn~~own as Foreign Shorthairs ~~in~~ the UK, and Oriental ~~Sh~~orthairs in the US.

A prize-winning Japanese Bobtail. This breed was first seen in the US in the early 1900s, when it was imported from Japan.

A litter of Siamese kittens. It will ~~b~~e a while before the color of ~~t~~heir face masks is fully ~~d~~eveloped.

In this book, all of the colors in a given breed will not be listed unless they are very limited in number. Once you decide on the breed of cat that you would like to own, and if you are really keen to know all about that breed, it is advisable to join the national breed club. You can also write to your chosen registration authority in order to obtain the official standard of the breed, which will detail all colors available.

Not all breeds have full recognition, for they may be in the process of becoming established. This is an important point to remember if you plan to exhibit cats. The newer breeds may not have championship status, so they cannot compete for titles.

The following sections may enable you to note the breeds that are likely to be of particular interest to you in the selection process for your eventual pet.

LONGHAIRED BREEDS

Balinese: This is a longhaired Siamese resulting from a natural mutation in the Siamese, not from an introduced gene.

The coat is not excessive and gives the cat softer lines than the Siamese. In the US, the only colors permitted are seal, chocolate, blue, and lilac. Other colors are termed

The Balinese is well muscled, lithe, and slender.

Javanese. In the UK, the latter would still be Balinese. This breed gained recognition during the 1970s.

Birman: Known as the "Sacred Cat of Burma." The coat is medium long, thus not too difficult to maintain. Breed features are the white paws and the darker points of the body. Colors are seal, blue, chocolate, and lilac, but others are possible. A very popular breed that arrived in Europe via France in 1919.

Lilac point Birman.

Established in the US during the late 1950s and in the UK during the 1960s.

Cymric: This is a longhaired Manx. The mutation appeared in North America during the 1960s. The coat is ample without being as woolly as in Persians. Not recognized in the UK.

Top: Cymric kitten. The Cymric is solidly constructed, with well-developed musculation. The coat is substantial but doesn't have the wool-like quality of the Persian. Below: Himalayan. This breed is also known as the Colourpoint Longhair or the Colorpoint Persian. In essence, it is a Persian with the markings of a Siamese.

Himalayan: This is the result of crossing Persians with Siamese. It is thus a Persian with colorpoint markings. In the UK, it is called a Colourpoint Longhair. Most American registries now regard it as a color variation of the Persian, all traces of Siamese having been bred out many years ago.

Javanese: This is a Balinese in non-accepted colors in that breed. It may be any color that is recognized in Colorpoint Shorthairs. Not regarded as a separate breed in the UK, but just one of the numerous variants of a Balinese.

Lilac point Javanese. This breed comes in all of the colors that are permitted for the Colorpoint Shorthair.

Kashmir: Few associations regard this Persian as a separate breed. It is actually a self-colored Himalayan, usually lilac or chocolate. In the UK, it is a Colourpoint Longhair and in most US registries, it is a color variety of the Persian.

Maine Coon: This is the oldest breed of longhaired cat in the US. It was very popular in the early days of cat shows at the turn of the century. After losing devotees following the importation of

Maine Coon. This popular breed from Down East sports a long, flowing coat accentuated by a thick ruff (the fur that encircles the neck). In a good specimen of the breed, the ears will have ample feathering. Rugged and hardy, Maine Coons are not fazed by Maine winters.

cat breeds

exotic Eastern breeds, it has now made a comeback and its numbers are rising steadily. Its origin is thought to be the result of crosses between Turkish cats and the short-haired breeds that pertained at the time. It is a good-sized feline that is hardy and available in most colors other than the pointed.

Nebelung: This is a longhaired Russian Blue which has group V recognition with The International Cat Association (TICA) of the US. This means that any outcrosses can be used in order to try and establish this hybrid as a breed.

Norwegian Forest: Very similar in appearance to the Maine Coon, but it is an older breed. Like its American counterpart, it is a hardy breed that will shed its coat (but not its plume-like tail)

during the warmer summer months. Not commonly seen outside of its Norwegian homeland. Not a recognized breed in the UK.

Persian: This breed, numerically, is probably the most popular purebred cat seen in Western countries. It arrived into Europe from Persia during the 16th century. In the UK, it was known simply as a French cat for many years. Its coat has been selectively bred for in order to make it very profuse. Its facial shape has changed as well over the years and is now more rounded, as are the eyes. Persians come in just about every color and pattern known to exist in cats. They are docile and affectionate but do require daily grooming if their beautiful coat is to remain as such. In the UK, they are simply called

Persian. In addition to their beauty and grace, Persians are gentle, affectionate cats that relish the attention of their human family. It's no wonder why they are as popular as they are.

longhaired cats, each color and coat pattern being regarded as a breed. Many other breeds originated from crosses to Persians in order to introduce the longhaired gene.

Ragdoll: The basis of this breed is its docile and affectionate nature. It is a new breed with limited acceptance in the US; it is not recognized in the UK. Three color types are accepted: bicolor, colorpoint, and mitted. The is not excessive so is easily managed.

Norwegian Forest, or Norsk Skaukatt. The appearance of this broad-chested, muscular breed appears somewhat similar to that of the Maine Coon. The thick coat covers a woolly undercoat.

Ragdoll, frost bi-color. One of the newer breeds in the fancy, Ragdolls have coats that are virtually non-matting. Their sweet expression is enhanced by their big blue eyes.

Siberian. This pedigreed Russian import made its way into the US from St. Petersburg in 1990. Its crowning glory is its magnificent coat.

This Ragdoll finds a sink a good place for a catnap.

The Turkish Angora, which originated in Ankara, Turkey, is known for its dense, silky coat. It is a progenitor of the present-day Persian. Turkish Angoras come in a number of attractive colors.

Siberian: One of the latest breeds to be introduced to the US, this is a very large cat of the Maine Coon type. It should prove to be both very hardy and popular with those liking big domestic felines.

Somali: This is a longhaired Abyssinian and is a very attractive breed. The longhair gene arose within the Abyssinian and is comparable to the Balinese in its effect. The tail is plume-like, but the body fur is of medium length—so is easily managed. A well-recommended breed.

Tiffanie: A longhaired Burmese. It has limited US recognition and none in the UK. There are no color restrictions, but it is to be assumed that these will be the same for the Burmese if the breed to gain international acceptance.

Turkish Angora: A very elegant and old breed originating in Ankara, Turkey. It known simply as the Angora in the UK. From crosses between this breed and the Persian, the present-day Persians arose. The fur is dense but silky. Although the original cats were pure white the breed is seen today in many colors, though in its homeland only pure whites are regarded as being true Angora. It is currently enjoying an upsurge in popularity in both the US and the UK

Somali. This long–haired version of the Abyssinian was created in the 1960s. Its three color varieties—red, ruddy, and blue—are enhanced by the soft, fine quality of the coat.

Turkish Van. The coloration of the Van is chalk white, accentuated by auburn markings. Not surprisingly, this breed, which was "discovered" in the Lake Van area of Turkey, is by no means water-shy.

breeders seek those breeds that are essentially un-changed from their original forms.

Turkish Van: This is a regional variety of the Angora but enjoys separate recognition in the UK. Its original color was white with auburn markings on the head and tail, but cream has now been accepted as a color for the markings. Like the Angora, it is very affectionate, enjoys water, and has a more manageable coat than does its cousin.

SHORTHAIRED BREEDS

Abyssinian: This very old breed first gained popularity in England during the 1870s. It was given its present name with the formation of the Abyssinian Cat Club in 1919. It is a noble-looking breed of foreign type that is available in the UK in a number of colors, but only in ruddy, red, blue, and fawn in the US.

The coat has a ticked effect, with the tips of the hairs being darker than the body color. There are also faint

Above: Abyssinian. This breed, which made its way from Abyssinia (now Ethiopia) to England in the 1860s, bears a resemblance to the African wild cat. The Abyssinian's four colors—red, ruddy, blue, and fawn—are enhanced by ticking. Abys are active, social cats that delight their owners with their antics. Below: American Curl, blue and white.

barrings on the legs and tail. A very intelligent feline, the Aby enjoys a select following. It is best suited to homes where its energetic nature is given an outlet.

American Curl: This is one of the newer breeds and is based on a dominant mutation that results in the ears turning outward to a greater or lesser degree. The body is of a soft foreign type. The hair is silky, and a longhaired variant is also in the making.

American Shorthair: This is the classic American equivalent to the very old British Shorthair. It is the regular street cat bred to a high level of quality over many generations. Tough and essentially unaltered over the years, the AS is everyone's idea of what a cat should look like. It is available in a wide range of colors and patterns. Not recognized in the UK.

American Wirehair: This breed is the result of a natural dominant mutation that appeared in 1966 in an American shorthair.

The fur is coarse, dense,

American Shorthair. The three tabby patterns in this breed are bold and sharply defined.

American Wirehair, red and white bi-color. Named for its coat, which is, of course, wiry, the American Wirehair is a cobby and muscular breed of cat.

and hard to the touch, being of a woolly nature. In all other respects, the breed may be regarded as an American shorthair, which is an allowable outcross at this time. Not recognized in the UK.

Bombay: This jet-black breed has a high gloss to its coat. Of foreign type, its development was begun in the 1970s and continues to this day. The parent breeds are the black American Shorthair and the sable Burmese. Of medium size, the Bombay

Bombay. The Bombay's satin-like black-as-coal coat and vivid copper eyes add to its unique appeal.

inherits all of the virtues of the two parent breeds, so it is hardy, intelligent, and very playful. Not recognized in the UK.

British Shorthair: This, in simple terms, is the street cat of Britain refined to a very high standard. Cobby in shape, hardy, and possessing a sleek but dense coat, the British Shorthair, as a purebred, dates back to the late 19th century, when the first cat shows were held. It is available in a wide range of colors and patterns, the

Burmese, sable. This breed, first recognized in 1936, is the result of a mating between a Siamese and a brown Oriental-type female. It is one of the ten most popular cat breeds in the US.

tabby, the spotted, and the blue being especially attractive. Tabby patterns are seen at their best in shorthaired breeds.

Burmese: This breed was established by a carefully planned program that paired Siamese with an import to the US that was of a brown foreign type. The result is a

cat that is lithe and oriental in appearance in the UK but somewhat more muscular in the US. The coat is short and exhibits a high sheen to it. The original color was sable (US), or seal (UK). There are now numerous colors accepted in the UK, but only sable, champagne, (chocolate UK), blue, and platinum (lilac UK) in the US. The breed is extremely intelligent and playful, so it is best suited to those who have the time to devote to it.

California Spangled: This breed has limited recognition in the US and none in the UK. It is a spotted breed developed by numerous crosses including the Abyssinian, Malayan,

Chartreux. One of the three blue breeds in the fancy, the Chartreux is a robust, well developed cat with a deep chest and well-developed shoulders. Its coat is medium-short, with just a trace of wooliness to it.

street cats, and others. It is an attractive breed available in a range of colors but is expensive.

Chartreux: The hallmark of this breed is its beautiful blue coat, which is plush and glossy. The tips of the hairs are silver.

The breed is French, though it is thought to carry British Blue bloodlines due to the decimation of the

British Shorthair, cream spotted tabby and white. The British Shorthair was first recognized as a breed in Great Britain in the late 19th century. It is the British counterpart to the American Shorthair.

56

cat breeds

Devon Rex. Like its "cousin," the Cornish Rex, the Devon Rex is a lively, active cat. Grooming—for both of these breeds—requires little more than gentle stroking with a soft cloth.

Colorpoint Shorthair, red point. In essence, this breed is a Siamese with points of any color other than those accepted for the Siamese by most US registries.

Chartreux during World War II. Its stature is that of European Shorthairs, and it has a quiet temperament. As with all blue breeds, it is a very imposing cat.

Colorpoint Shorthair: This breed is recognized by some associations, while being regarded purely as a color variant of the Siamese by others, notably the British. It is a Siamese in colors other than seal, blue, chocolate, or lilac. The additional colors, such as red, cream, tabby, and tortie point, were introduced from other breeds, thus the division over their acceptance as being Siamese. Any other breeds used in transferring color have long been bred out, so the breed can best be regarded as a Siamese.

Cornish and Devon Rexes: These breeds arose from independent mutations that appeared in British pet cats from 1950 to 1960.

The mutations creating the wavy pattern in the fur are at differing locations, which is why they are separate breeds. If they are interbred, only normal-haired cats will result. The fur is soft and curly,

Cornish Rex. The curly coat, which is the result of a mutation, is soft and has a silky texture.

while the conformation is of the foreign type.

Rexes are available in a wide range of colors and are delightful felines that are very striking in appearance. They are not to everyone's taste, however. They should be protected from very cold and damp weather, as their coats are not as resilient as those of normal cats.

Egyptian Mau: If you like spotted cats, then the Mau is one of the breeds you could select from. It is an interesting

Egyptian Mau. This breed is available in a number of colors, each of which is accented by markings, including a dorsal stripe, heavily ringed tail, and necklaces.

58

Japanese Bobtail. The bobtail can vary somewhat in length from specimen to specimen. In Japan, the bi-color and tri-color varieties are considered by many to be good luck charms.

Exotic Shorthair: When Persians are crossed with American Shorthairs, the result is the Exotic Shorthair. The object of the original breeders was to produce an American Shorthair that had both a denser fur and a more Persian look to it. The Exotic is a variable breed in its coat quality and is a very well-muscled cat with a short muzzle, giving it a distinctive facial expression: snub nosed. Crosses back to American Shorthairs and Persians are still allowed at this time.

Havana Brown: This breed is known simply as the Havana in the UK, where the breed was first developed during the 1950s. It is the result of crosses between Siamese, British Shorthairs, and Russian Blues. In the UK, the breed is very Siamese in appearance, but in the US it is now more foreign in confor-

Korat. It is believed that the origins of this silver-blue beau trace back centuries ago Thailand (formerly Siam). In good specimen of the breed, t eye color is a vivid shade of green

Manx, the tailless cat of Britain, the bobtail is not linked to any known abnorr side effects. The breed gaine recognition in the US aroun

Manx, or Cat of the Isle of Ma The Manx is completely tailles in fact, there is an actual hollo where the tail would norma begin.

breed that was first imported into the US in 1956 from Italy. Its origin is Cairo, Egypt. Its type is broadly foreign, and the quality of its spots are

Havana Brown. This breed, available in a variety of shades of chestnut brown, is the result of a cross between a seal point Siamese and a black Shorthair. Havana fanciers rave about its intelligence and playful personality.

variable. A well-marked individual is most impressive. The colors available are silver, bronze, smoke, and pewter, but dilutions of them are possible to produce blue or lilac for example. Not recognized in the UK.

mation, resembling the Russian Blue in its stature. The color is of course dark brown.

Japanese Bobtail: The short tail is the main feature of this cat of foreign appearance. However, unlike the

1971, though it was evident the US for many years prior this.

The colors are numerous, but the bi- and tri-colored examples are those most favored. An interesting bree that has steadily increased i

Exotic Shorthair. This sturdy-looking breed is the result of a cross between a Persian and an American Shorthair. The plush, dense coat is silky in texture.

Ocicat, chocolate. The distinctive spotted pattern is the hallmark of this hybrid breed. The Ocicat is named for the ocelot, which it resembles.

numbers over the years.

Korat: This breed hails from Thailand (formerly Siam) and is the third of the blue breeds so far discussed from which you can choose. It is the least well-known of the blue breeds quartet and has a heart-shaped face. However, its popularity has slowly increased in recent years. Its conformation is of foreign type and it makes for a charming pet.

Malayan: In the registries that regard this cat as a breed, it is a Burmese of any color other than sable. It thus has the same build and lively nature as the Burmese. Not recognized in the UK as a separate breed.

Manx: This is the famed tailless cat from the Isle of Man in Great Britain. Not all Manx cats are born tailless, some have tails of variable

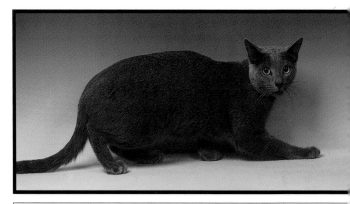

Russian Blue. In some registries, a lighter shade of blue is preferred; others the darker the blue, the better. Luminous green eyes lend to tł Russian Blue's physical appeal.

Oriental Shorthair. This breed is an example of what is known in the fancy as *foreign type*: Slim, long legged, and head tapered into a wedge shape.

length. The tailless mutation is linked to spinal and other abnormalities, so caution is strongly advised before considering this cat. Its conformation resembles that of the British Shorthair, and it is available in a very wide range of colors and coat patterns.

Manx -to-Manx matings result in 25% lethality in the potential offspring.

Ocicat: This recent breed came about purely by chance in an Abyssinian x Siamese litter. The result was so fascinating that a breeding program was begun, and the Ocicat is the result. It is a wild-looking feline with a gorgeous spotted coat that can be seen in a number of colors. It is also quite a big cat, and these facts have made the breed extremely desirable. It makes a delightful pet, but if you choose the Ocicat, watch out for it as it makes a tempting target for cat thieves. It is presently not recognized in the UK.

Oriental Shorthair: This breed, in the US, is a Siamese in any self color, such as blue, red, cream, or chestnut. These would be regarded as Foreign Shorthairs in the UK. In both the UK and the US, the Orientals also include the tabby pattern, the particolors, and the shaded colors, such as blue smoke. The breed has the same inquisitive nature and intelligence as the Siamese, of which it can

be regarded as a color varia

Russian Blue: This gorgeous breed is, of course, blue, and it is the most popular of the breeds of thi color. Its body is of a mildly foreign type, and its history dates back for a few centuries. It was one of the first cats to be exhibited when c shows first came into being Great Britain during the la 19th century. In the UK, th breed remains lithe in shap whereas in the US, it is ratl more muscular and the fac

The Scottish Fold is a unique with a bright, sweet temperame

cat breeds

Siamese littermates, seal point and blue point. In conformation, the Siamese is fine-boned, with slender legs.

traditionally seen in four colors: seal, chocolate, blue, and lilac. In its longhaired form, it is known as the Balinese; and in its non-pointed form, it is called either a Foreign Shorthair or an Oriental shorthair.

It is an extremely intelligent feline that is both mischievous and very playful. It is also a cat that uses its voice quite a lot, so will "talk" to you continually. The breed has been used to create many other breeds. Only the Persian enjoys greater popularity. There are many specialist clubs and shows devoted to the Siamese.

Singapura: This is one of the more recent breeds and hails from Singapore. It is a moderately sized cat of foreign type.

Its color is agouti, meaning its fur is ticked. The ground color is ivory, and there are at least two tick bars in a dark brown. There are faint barrings on the tail and legs. Not recognized in the UK.

Snowshoe: This is one of

The Snowshoe is the result of a cross between Siamese and bi-colored American Shorthairs. It is named for the white color pattern on its feet. The Snowshoe is one of the newer breeds to emerge in the cat fancy.

the numerous developing breeds in the US. It is produced by crossing bi-colored American Shorthairs with Siamese, then either inter-breeding with the offspring, or mating back to Siamese. The objective is to produce a cat of a very loose foreign type that has white paws and points. The latter means the body fur is of a lighter shade than that of the lower legs. The present colors are seal point or blue

ore rounded. The coat is .ort, dense, and very plush.
Scottish Fold: The fold .utation results in the tips of .e ears folding forward. This .es the breed its character-ic, and not unpleasant, .ial appearance. The muta-.n occurred in a Scottish cat 1961. Although the breed .s recognition in most .untries, its homeland of the . is not among them. This is because the muta-.n, in homozygous form (if th parents of a litter are .ld cats), adversely affects .e legs, tail, and spinal .umn. This being so, Folds .ould always be mated to .rmal American or British .orthairs. The breed is .ailable in a wide range of .ors and patterns.
Siamese: This breed is .own to people all over the .rld. It made its Western .pearance at the very first . show in England in 1871. .vas improved by the addi-.n of high-quality stock .en by the King of Siam .ailand) to friends in Britain .l the US. The Siamese is

The Singapura, which originated in Singapore, received US recognition in 1988. Its coloration is ivory accented by agouti ticking. The coat is short and has a fine texture.

point. In appearance, the bre
is somewhat like a Ragdoll or
Birman; but it has shorter ha
and more white on the body.

Sphynx: This breed is
unusual in that it is hairless
Actually, it does have hair,
but there is so little of it tha
it appears bald. It is of foreig
type, and the present mutation appeared in Canada in
1966. The breed is not recog
nized in the UK.

Tonkinese: This breed is
the result of crossing a
Siamese with a Burmese. It
of a type intermediate between the two and is seen in
five colors at this time: natu
ral mink (mid brown), cham
pagne mink (light brown),
blue mink, honey mink, and
platinum mink (silver gray).
is not recognized in the UK.
is a nice breed for those whe
like the two parent breeds b
would prefer to see a bit mo.
body on them.

For those who seek
the truly unusual in
a cat, the Sphynx is
a top contender.
This hairless breed
comes in a number
of colors and is said
to make a devoted
companion cat.

The Tonkinese, a
hybrid of Siamese
and Burmese origin,
is available in
various shades of
mink. In personality,
these medium-sized
cats are outgoing
and friendly.